My Best Book of

Spaceships

Ian Graham

KING*f*ISHER

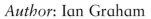

Author: Ian Graham
Managing Editor: Camilla Hallinan
Series Editor: Sue Nicholson
Illustrators: Gary Bines,
 Lee Gibbons, Ceri Llewellyn
Art Editor: Ch'en-Ling
Art Director and cover design:
 Terry Woodley
Series Designer: Ben White

Photographs on p26 by Martin
 Redfern/NASA

Production Controller: Kelly Johnson
Printed in Hong Kong

KINGFISHER
Kingfisher Publications Plc
New Penderel House,
283-288 High Holborn,
London WC1V 7HZ

First published by Kingfisher Publications Plc 1998
First published in paperback 2000
(hb) 10 9 8 7 6 5 4 3

3TR/0499/WKT/MA/128KMA

(pb) 10 9 8 7 6 5 4 3 2 1

1TR/0500/WKT/MA/128KMA

A CIP catalogue record for this book is
available from the British Library.

ISBN 0 7534 0216 5 (hb)
ISBN 0 7534 0466 4 (pb)

Contents

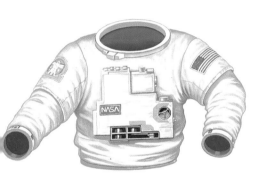

Looking into space

For thousands of years, people have gazed in wonder at the night sky. Slowly, they learned more and more about the twinkling stars and the planets above them. Many dreamed of visiting and exploring the planets, but there was no way of travelling there. Instead, people had to make do with fuzzy views seen through telescopes.

Nowadays, we have all kinds of spacecraft that can travel into space, visit the planets, and even land on them.

Pathfinder explorer on Mars

Robot explorers
Robot explorers have become our eyes and ears on distant worlds we have not yet visited ourselves.

What's in space?

The Earth is one of nine planets that fly through space around the Sun. The path each planet follows as it flies around the Sun is called an orbit. The Earth takes a year to orbit the Sun once. The Sun is enormous. A million Earths could fit inside it with lots of room to spare.

Mercury
The closest planet to the Sun

The Sun
The star at the centre of our Solar System

Venus
A boiling hot planet where it rains acid

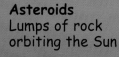

Asteroids
Lumps of rock orbiting the Sun

The pull of gravity
Gravity is an invisible force that pulls things towards it. The Sun is so big, its pull of gravity is strong enough to hold all the planets in their orbits.

Stars
The Sun and stars we can see from Earth are part of a huge group, or galaxy, called the Milky Way

Earth's moon

Earth
Our home planet

Mars
A red and rocky planet

Jupiter
The biggest planet in the Solar System

The Solar System
The Solar System is the name given to the Sun's family. It includes the planets and their moons, comets, and all the lumps of rock, dust and ice that orbit the Sun.

Pluto
The farthest
planet from
the Sun

Comet
A lump of icy rock that
sprouts a bright tail
as it nears the Sun

Neptune
A beautiful blue
planet streaked
with white clouds

Saturn
A planet surrounded
by beautiful rings

Uranus
A planet
tipped over
on its side

Far, far beyond our
galaxy are other
galaxies containing
billions of stars

Rocket power

A rocket blasts off from its launch pad and soars into the sky with flames streaming from its engines. As it climbs higher and higher, the air around it becomes thinner and thinner until there is none at all. The rocket has reached space.

Blast-off!

When people wanted to launch machines into space, they had to invent rockets to carry them there. Only rockets are powerful enough to escape the 'pull' of Earth's gravity.

Staging

A rocket is made up of
parts called stages. When
each stage has used up its
fuel, it is dropped to save
weight. The rest of the rocket
carries on into space.

Spacecraft

The top of the rocket then
opens and a spacecraft
comes out. Some spacecraft
circle Earth. Others are
carried deeper into space,
by more powerful rockets.

Apollo spacecraft

Saturn V
Height: 111m
Carried Apollo spacecraft and astronauts to the Moon between 1969 and 1972

All kinds of rocket

Every spacecraft and satellite sent into space has been carried there by a rocket. The first rockets were quite small, and could only lift a small weight. So the first spacecraft and satellites had to be small, too. As people learned more about how to make rockets and how to launch them, the rockets became bigger and more powerful. Bigger rockets can launch bigger spacecraft.

The biggest rocket ever built was the American Saturn V Moon rocket. (The 'V' stands for '5'.)

Ariane 4
Height: 54–58m
Since 1981, Ariane rockets have launched over 100 satellites from French Guiana in South America

Vostok spacecraft

Mercury spacecraft

Redstone
Height: 25m
Carried the Mercury spacecraft and the first American astronauts into space between 1961 and 1963

A-class
Height: 34m
Carried the first Russian satellite into space in 1957, the first living creature (a dog called Laika) also in 1957 and, in 1961, the first human being – Yuri Gagarin

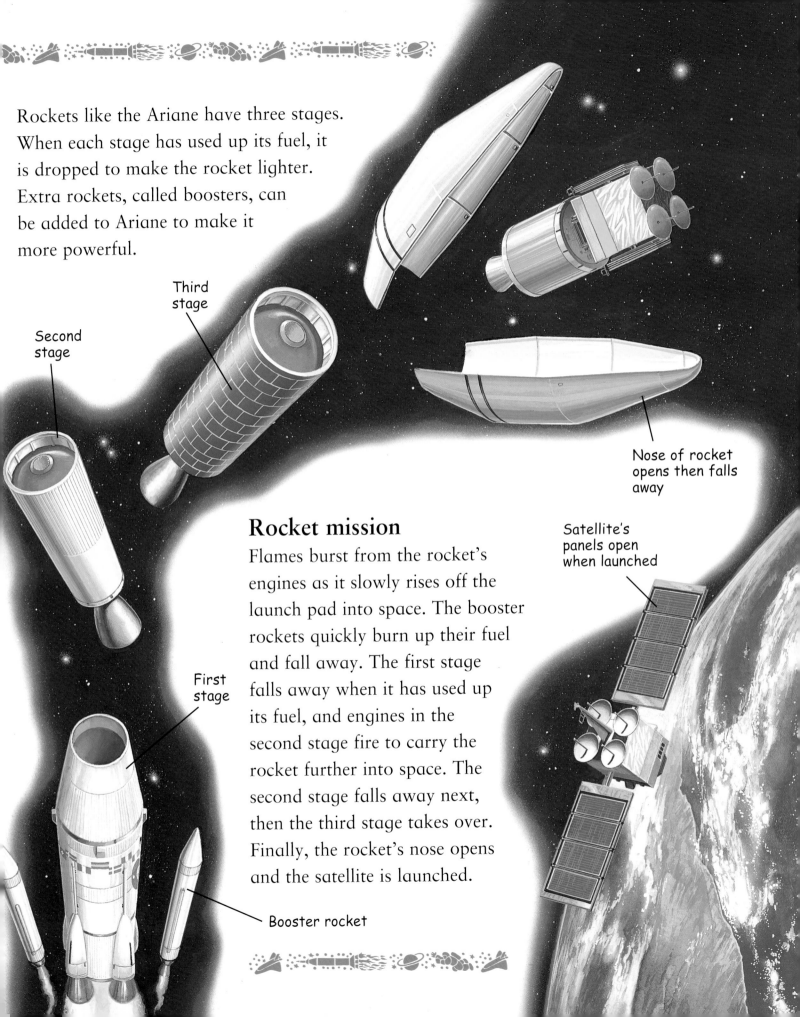

Rockets like the Ariane have three stages.
When each stage has used up its fuel, it
is dropped to make the rocket lighter.
Extra rockets, called boosters, can
be added to Ariane to make it
more powerful.

Third
stage

Second
stage

Nose of rocket
opens then falls
away

Rocket mission

Satellite's
panels open
when launched

Flames burst from the rocket's
engines as it slowly rises off the
launch pad into space. The booster
rockets quickly burn up their fuel
and fall away. The first stage
falls away when it has used up
its fuel, and engines in the
second stage fire to carry the
rocket further into space. The
second stage falls away next,
then the third stage takes over.
Finally, the rocket's nose opens
and the satellite is launched.

First
stage

Booster rocket

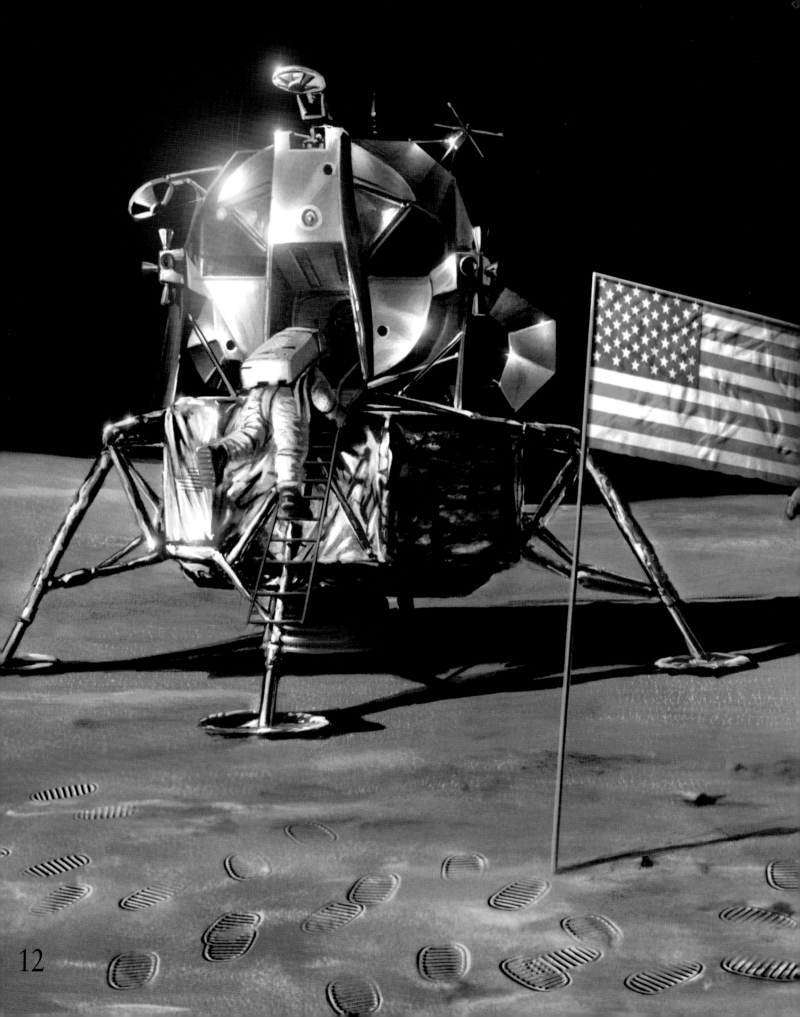

Going to the Moon

In July 1969, millions of people all over the world turned on their television sets at the same time. They were watching something that had never ever been seen before – an astronaut climbing out of a spacecraft that had just landed on the Moon. It was the first time that anyone from Earth had walked on another world.

◀ When the astronaut Neil Armstrong stepped on to the dusty surface of the Moon, he was farther away from home than any other explorer had ever been.

Moon Buggy

On later Moon missions, astronauts took a special car to the Moon called a Lunar Rover, or Moon Buggy. It helped them get around the Moon's rocky surface more easily.

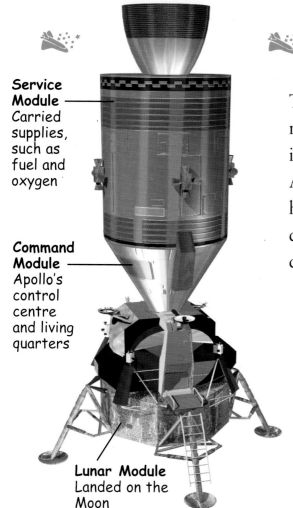

Service Module
Carried supplies, such as fuel and oxygen

Command Module
Apollo's control centre and living quarters

Lunar Module
Landed on the Moon

The Moon is our closest neighbour in space, but it is still 400,000km away. Altogether, 27 astronauts have flown to the Moon, and 12 have landed on its dusty, rocky surface.

Apollo spacecraft

The Apollo spacecraft was made up of three parts called modules. The Lunar Module was the only part of the spacecraft that landed on the Moon. The Command Module was the only part that came back to Earth. The spacecraft had to carry everything the astronauts needed for their mission – including the air they breathed.

Apollo Moon mission

◁ Flames shot from the five engines at the bottom of the huge Saturn V rocket. Then it slowly rose off the launch pad and climbed into the sky. The deafening roar from its engines made the ground shake.

▲ Three hours after take-off, the Command and Service Modules separated from the Saturn V rocket. They turned around and joined with the Lunar Module.

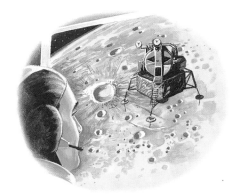

3 The Apollo spacecraft then carried on into space. It took three days for the astronauts to journey to the Moon.

4 Two astronauts floated down a tunnel into the Lunar Module and flew it to the Moon. The third stayed in the Command Module.

5 The astronauts explored the Moon's surface and collected rocks. They also raised the American flag. There is no breeze on the Moon, so the flag was held open by a stiff wire. The flag – and the astronauts' footprints – are still on the Moon.

Moon rocks

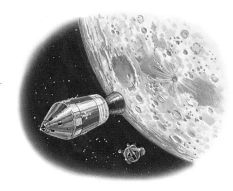

6 To leave the Moon, the Lunar Module split in two. Its top half blasted off, using the bottom as a launch pad.

7 The Lunar Module linked with the Command Module. It was then cut loose because it wasn't needed any more.

8 The Command Module separated from the Service Module. It glowed brightly in the sky as it entered the air around Earth. Parachutes opened to slow it down before it splashed into the sea. The crew was soon picked up by a waiting ship.

Shuttle power

Most rockets and spacecraft are used only once. This is an incredibly expensive way of sending machines and people into space – no one would build a jumbo jet and throw it away after only one flight. A rocket-powered spacecraft called a Space Shuttle is different because it can be used over and over again. It blasts off from a launch pad like a rocket, but lands on a runway like an aeroplane.

Space junk

Space junk is a serious problem for astronauts working in space. Parts of old rockets and broken satellites still orbit Earth. If they collide, the fuel inside them may explode, sending pieces of metal flying in all directions.

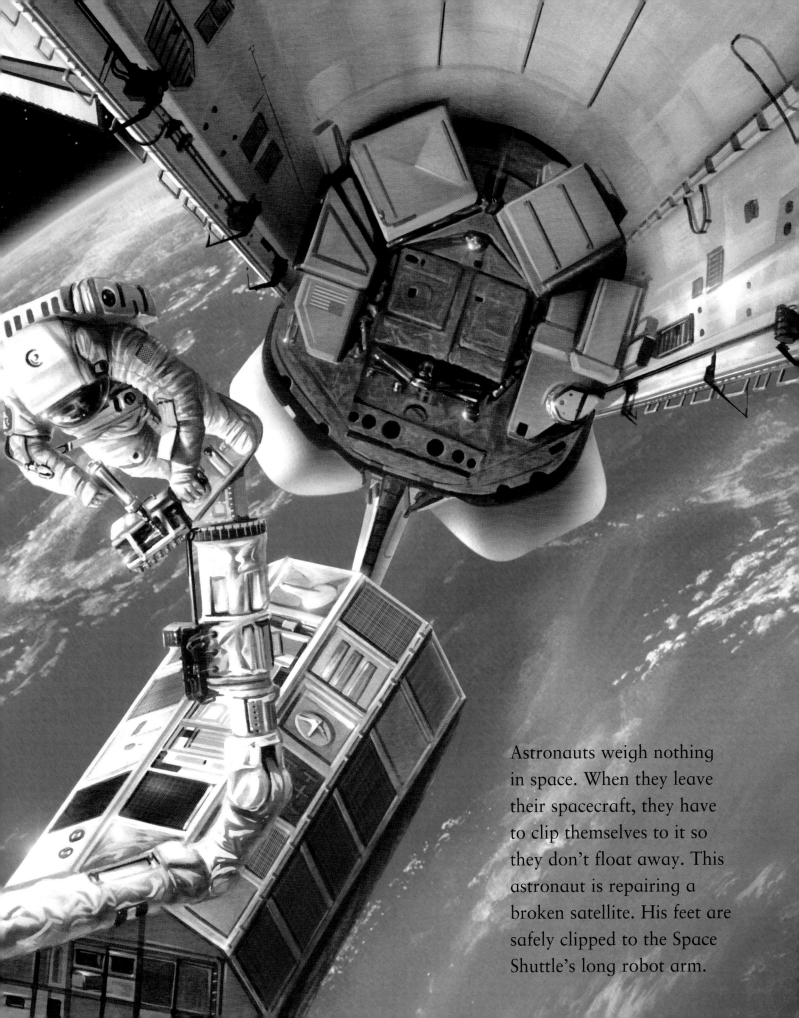

Astronauts weigh nothing in space. When they leave their spacecraft, they have to clip themselves to it so they don't float away. This astronaut is repairing a broken satellite. His feet are safely clipped to the Space Shuttle's long robot arm.

The Space Shuttle

The Shuttle is one of the most complicated machines ever built. There is nothing else like it. It can fly in the air like an aircraft and also in space like a rocket.

External fuel tank

Booster rocket

Flight deck

Orbiter

The main part of the Shuttle is a spacecraft with wings called the Orbiter. It is carried into space by three large rocket engines and two booster rockets.

Payload bay (doors closed)

Wings

Tail fin

Rocket engines

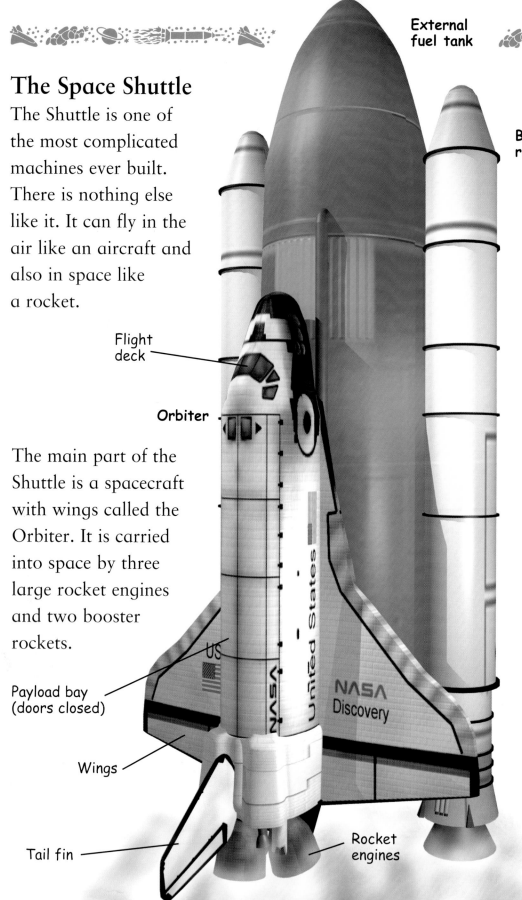

Satellite

Robot arm helps move satellites

Payload bay (doors open)

The Space Shuttle carries satellites into space in its payload bay. Sometimes it brings broken satellites back to Earth for repair. On some missions, it carries a laboratory called the Spacelab, in which scientists do experiments in space.

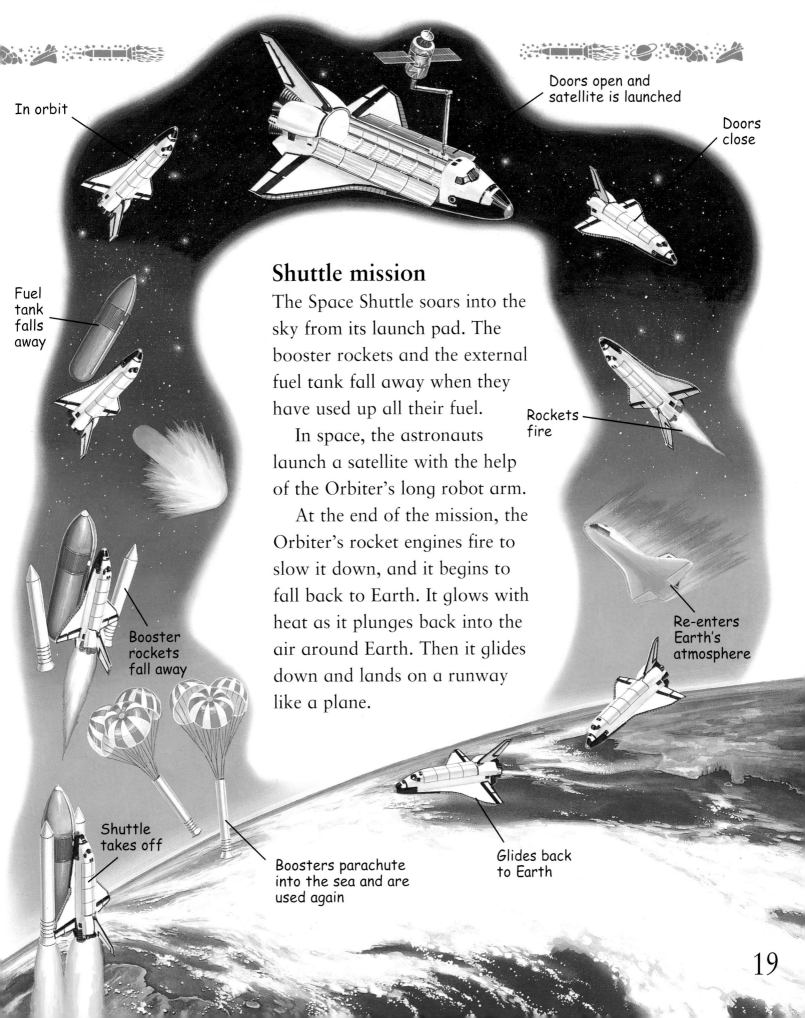

In orbit

Doors open and satellite is launched

Doors close

Fuel tank falls away

Rockets fire

Shuttle mission

The Space Shuttle soars into the sky from its launch pad. The booster rockets and the external fuel tank fall away when they have used up all their fuel.

In space, the astronauts launch a satellite with the help of the Orbiter's long robot arm.

At the end of the mission, the Orbiter's rocket engines fire to slow it down, and it begins to fall back to Earth. It glows with heat as it plunges back into the air around Earth. Then it glides down and lands on a runway like a plane.

Re-enters Earth's atmosphere

Booster rockets fall away

Shuttle takes off

Boosters parachute into the sea and are used again

Glides back to Earth

19

Spacesuits

In space there is no air. Anything the Sun shines on is boiling hot, and anything in the shade is freezing cold. Human beings cannot live in space. We need air to breathe and we need to be at the right temperature – not too hot, and not too cold.

A spacecraft has to provide astronauts with air to breathe, and it has to keep them warm. When astronauts leave the spacecraft, they must wear a spacesuit, which does the same job.

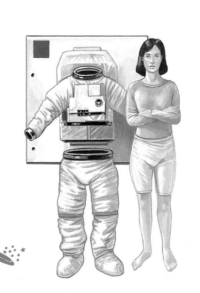

Gas thruster

Adjustable arm

Hand controller

Nitrogen gas tank

Gas thruster

TV camera

Life-support backpack

Manned Manoeuvring Unit (MMU) helps astronauts fly around outside the Shuttle

Putting on a spacesuit

This spacesuit is called the Space Shuttle EMU, which is short for Extravehicular Mobility Unit. The suit has a special backpack which keeps fresh air flowing through the suit.

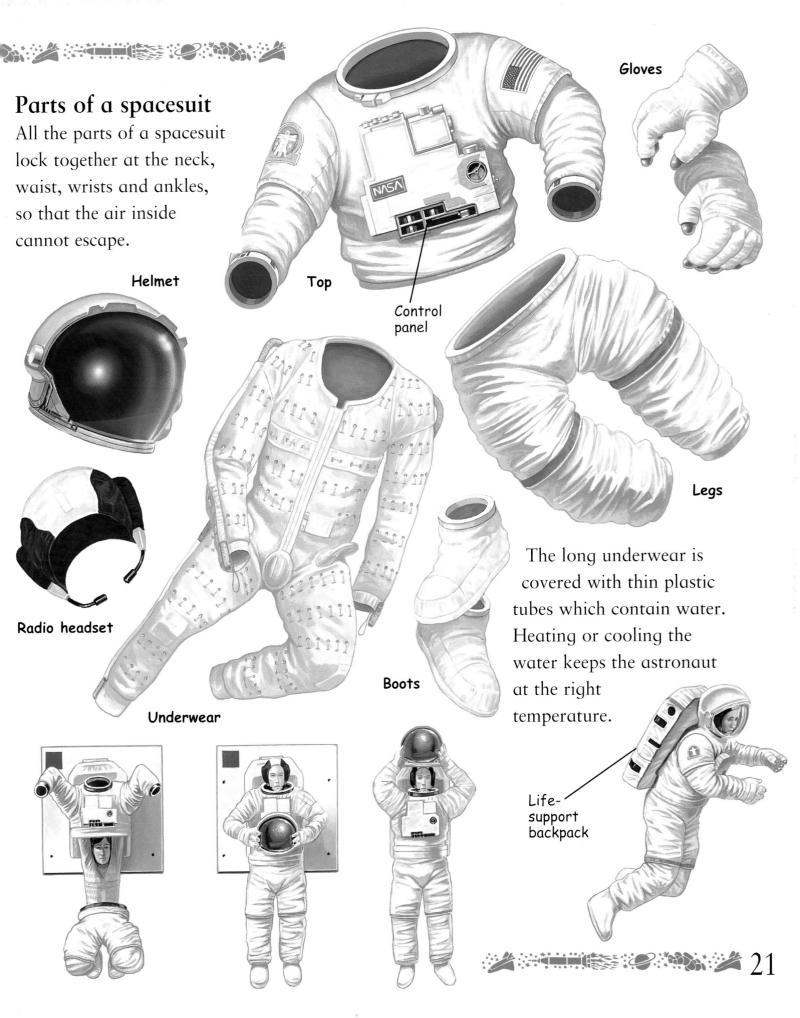

Parts of a spacesuit

All the parts of a spacesuit lock together at the neck, waist, wrists and ankles, so that the air inside cannot escape.

Gloves

Helmet

Top

Control panel

Legs

Radio headset

The long underwear is covered with thin plastic tubes which contain water. Heating or cooling the water keeps the astronaut at the right temperature.

Underwear

Boots

Life-support backpack

Working in space

Every day's work on board the Space Shuttle is set out in the flight plan for the mission. A typical mission may take ten days.

▶ In space, everything and everyone in the Shuttle is weightless. So if an astronaut drops a pen, it doesn't fall to the ground. It simply floats in the air.

Strawberries

Vanilla pudding

Lemonade

Vegetables

Potatoes

Beef steak

▶ Sleeping bags are stuck to the cabin walls so they don't float around. The astronauts wear a mask to block out the light. They are woken by music, beamed up from Earth.

▲ Shuttle astronauts have about 100 different kinds of food to choose from. Some food is dried and has to be mixed with water. Drinks are sucked through tubes so drops of liquid don't float around the cabin.

Space Shuttle toilet

◀ Astronauts have to clip themselves to the seat when they use the toilet, or they might float away.

The Shuttle carries up to seven people. The commander, in the left seat, is in charge of the spacecraft. The pilot helps the commander.

Mission specialists are trained to do a particular job on the mission, such as launching a satellite.

The commander, pilot and mission specialists are all astronauts. Extra crew members, called payload specialists, are not. They may be scientists or doctors who do experiments in the Spacelab, or engineers who operate special equipment.

Eyes in space

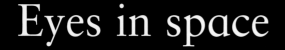

A satellite floats silently in space, its camera pointing at the swirling clouds of a violent hurricane far below. Weather satellites watch the Earth and its weather all day and night. Other satellites beam telephone calls and television programmes all over the world. There are hundreds of satellites orbiting Earth. They have become so important, it's difficult to imagine our world without them.

Navigational satellite

Weather satellite

▲ Even though they are far away in space, weather satellites can measure the temperature of the land and sea, the speed of the wind and even the height of waves.

24

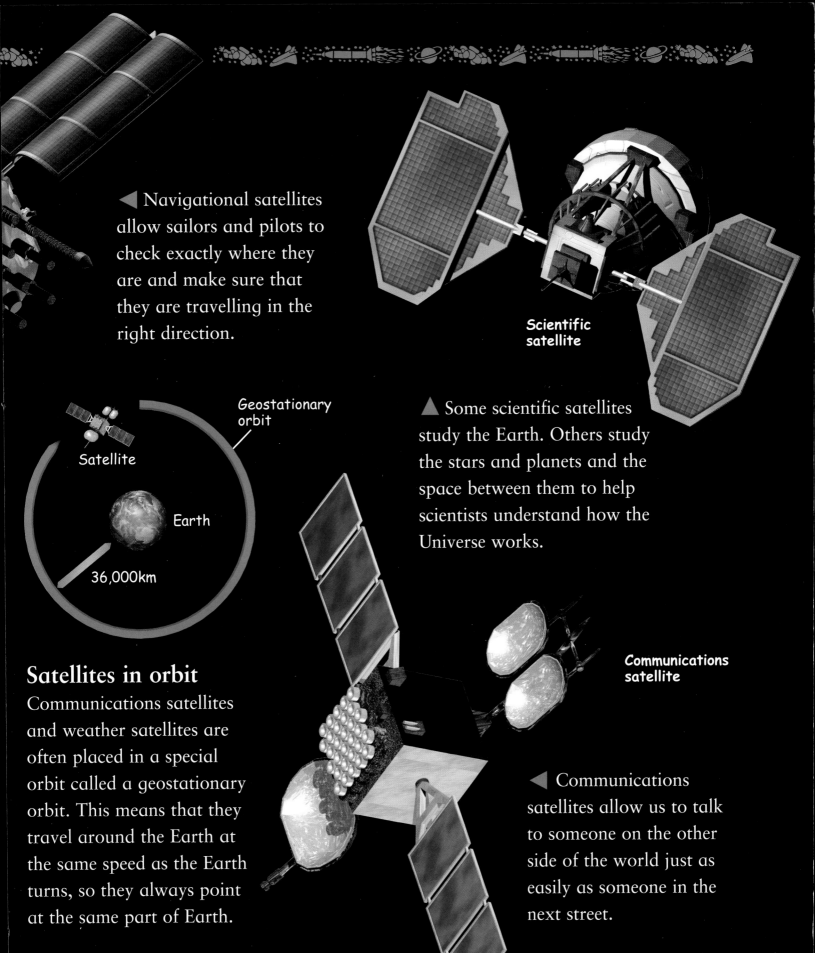

◀ Navigational satellites allow sailors and pilots to check exactly where they are and make sure that they are travelling in the right direction.

Scientific satellite

Geostationary orbit

Satellite

Earth

36,000km

▲ Some scientific satellites study the Earth. Others study the stars and planets and the space between them to help scientists understand how the Universe works.

Communications satellite

Satellites in orbit

Communications satellites and weather satellites are often placed in a special orbit called a geostationary orbit. This means that they travel around the Earth at the same speed as the Earth turns, so they always point at the same part of Earth.

◀ Communications satellites allow us to talk to someone on the other side of the world just as easily as someone in the next street.

The Hubble Telescope

Stars look so beautiful because they twinkle like diamonds, but twinkling makes it difficult for astronomers to see them clearly through a telescope. Twinkling is caused by swirling streams of warm and cold air around the Earth bending the starlight this way and that.

A telescope in space has the best view of the stars, because there is no air to make them twinkle. The biggest telescope in space is the Hubble Space Telescope, which was launched from the Space Shuttle in 1990.

Repairing the Hubble

When the Hubble was launched, astronomers discovered that its view was blurred because it had a faulty mirror. Shuttle astronauts mended the telescope in 1993. Since then, the Hubble has been sending clear pictures back to Earth.

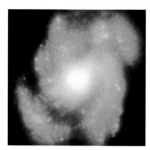

Before repair

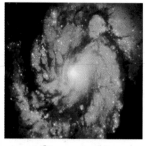

After repair

▶ The Hubble has two large, flat solar panels – one on each side. These make electricity from sunlight to power the Hubble's instruments. It sends its pictures to Earth by radio.

Space probes

Every 175 years, the giant planets Jupiter, Saturn, Uranus and Neptune line up. This means a spacecraft can visit all of them in one trip. Two space probes, Voyagers 1 and 2, travelled all the way to these planets. They sent back some of the most beautiful pictures we have ever seen – of stormy orange and white clouds over Jupiter, volcanoes erupting on Jupiter's moons and the broad, flat rings around Saturn.

Journey to the stars

Tiny space probes – some no bigger than a shoebox – have visited every planet in the Solar System except Pluto. A few have even left the Solar System altogether. Pioneer 10 is the farthest away. Since it was launched in 1972, it has travelled ten thousand million kilometres from Earth. It will not reach another star for eight million years!

Mariner

Mariner 9 orbited Mars in 1971, and Mariner 10 visited Venus and Mercury in 1974.

▲ The Voyager probes carry discs with pictures and sounds from Earth in case they are found by beings from another world.

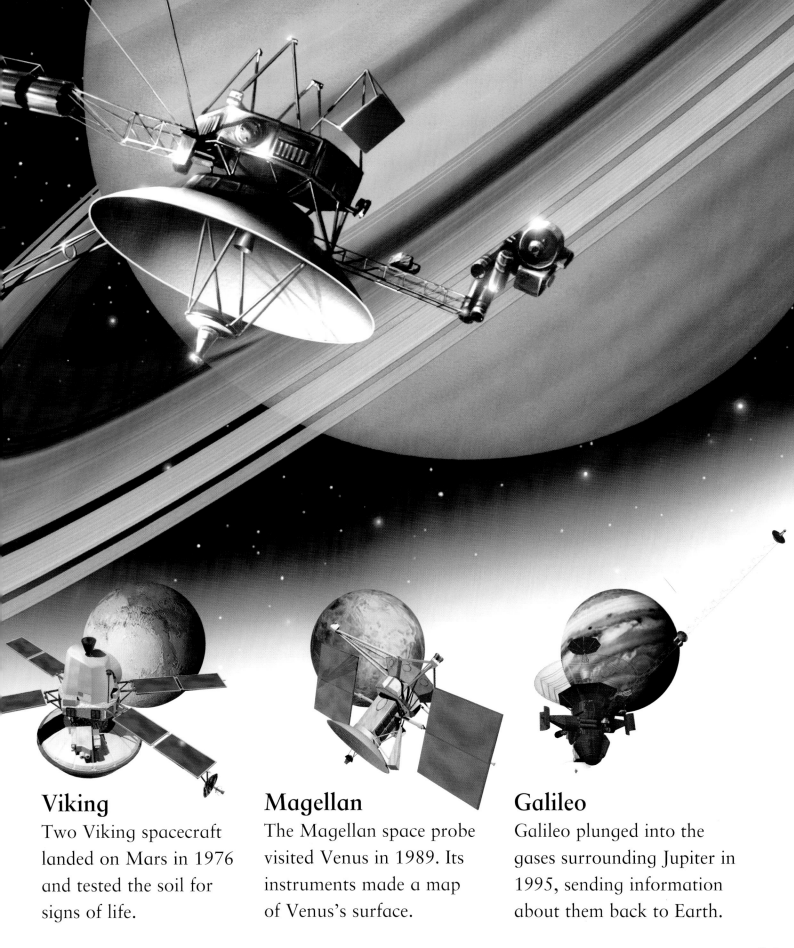

Viking
Two Viking spacecraft landed on Mars in 1976 and tested the soil for signs of life.

Magellan
The Magellan space probe visited Venus in 1989. Its instruments made a map of Venus's surface.

Galileo
Galileo plunged into the gases surrounding Jupiter in 1995, sending information about them back to Earth.

Space stations

In the future, astronauts will visit the planets. Perhaps people will even live on Mars. But before this can happen, engineers need to learn how to build spacecraft for flights lasting years instead of days or weeks, and scientists need to study how very long spaceflights affect astronauts. The first step is to build a large space station in orbit around Earth.

Space Station Freedom

A new International Space Station will be built over the new few years. It will be home to teams of scientists and engineers who will learn how to live and work in space.

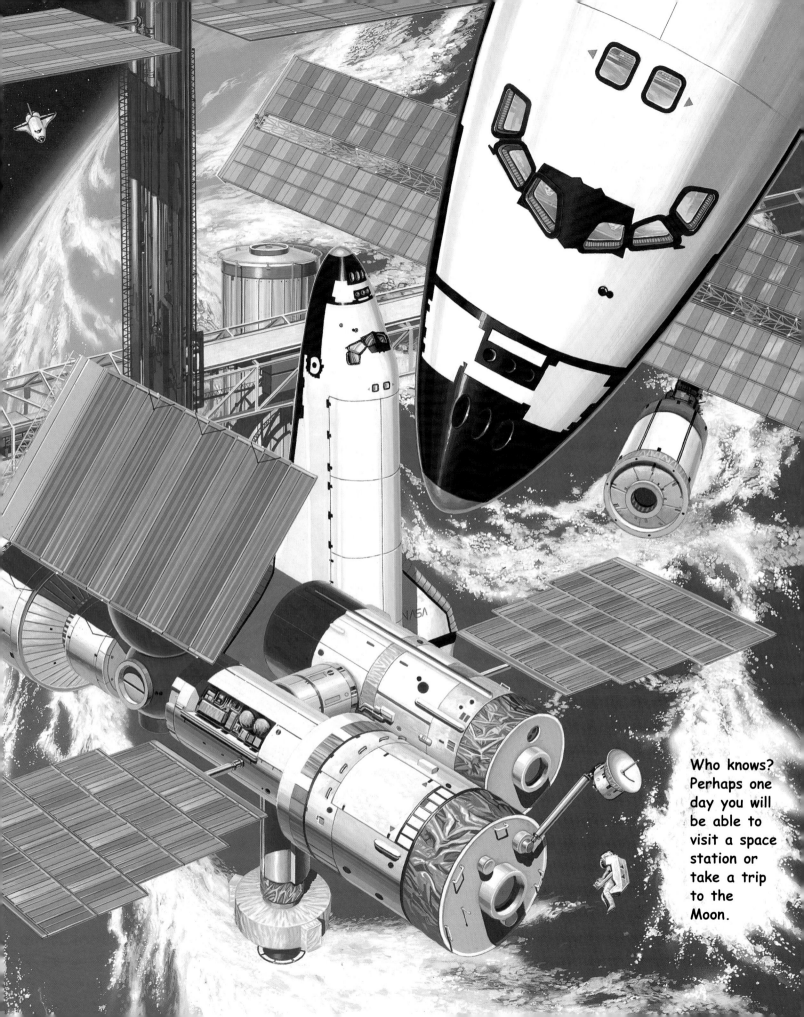

Who knows? Perhaps one day you will be able to visit a space station or take a trip to the Moon.

Glossary

astronaut A space traveller.

atmosphere The layer of gases that surround a planet or moon. Earth's atmosphere, or air, is made mostly of three gases – nitrogen, oxygen and carbon dioxide.

booster An extra rocket used to help launch a larger rocket or the Space Shuttle.

capsule A small spacecraft with just enough room inside to fit in the crew.

countdown The preparations for the launch of a rocket as a clock ticks backwards to zero, the moment when the rocket fires and takes off.

EVA Extra Vehicular Activity – another name for a spacewalk.

gravity The force that pulls everything down to the ground and keeps the planets in orbit around the Sun, and satellites in orbit around planets.

launch pad The platform a rocket or Space Shuttle stands on for take-off.

moon A small world that orbits a planet. Every planet apart from Mercury and Venus has at least one moon. A moon is a natural satellite.

Moon Buggy An electric car used by some of the Apollo astronauts to drive around on the Moon.

NASA The National Aeronautics and Space Administration – an organization that runs American spaceflights.

orbit The path of a satellite around a planet, or a planet around the Sun.

payload Cargo carried by a rocket or the Space Shuttle.

planet A world in orbit around the Sun.

re-entry Coming back into, or re-entering, the Earth's atmosphere from space.

satellite An object in orbit around a planet. A moon is a natural satellite. A spacecraft is an artificial satellite.

Solar System The Sun and everything that orbits it, including the planets, their moons, asteroids and comets.

space probe An unmanned spacecraft sent far away from Earth to find out more about the Sun, the planets or their moons.

spaceship Any spacecraft that carries people.

space station A large manned spacecraft that is kept in space for several years.

spacesuit The special clothes worn by astronauts to protect them when they go outside their spacecraft.

splashdown Landing a spacecraft in the sea.

thruster A tiny rocket engine fired to nudge a spacecraft into a new position.